▶ Volume 86 of
the Yale Series
of Younger Poets

Bears
Dancing
in the
Northern
Air

CHRISTIANE JACOX KYLE

FOREWORD BY JAMES DICKEY

YALE UNIVERSITY

PRESS

NEW HAVEN

AND LONDON

Publication of this volume was made possible by a grant from the Guinzburg Fund.

Designed by Nancy Ovedovitz. Set in Bembo type by Brevis Press. Printed in the United States of America.

Library of Congress Cataloging-in-Publication Data
Jacox Kyle, Christiane, 1950–
Bears dancing in the northern air / Christiane Jacox Kyle ; foreword by James Dickey.
    p.   cm. — (Yale series of younger poets ; v. 86)
ISBN 0-300-05007-0 (cloth). — ISBN 0-300-05008-9 (paper)
I. Title.   II. Series.
PS3560.A285B44   1991
811'.54—dc20   90-23664
                                                    CIP

The paper in this book meets the guidelines for permanence and durability of the Committee on Production Guidelines for Book Longevity of the Council on Library Resources.

10   9   8   7   6   5   4   3   2   1

For my father and mother,
and Charles and Katherine
in whom love is renewed
again and again

"The human voice is like a cracked cauldron on which we beat our tune for bears to dance, while all the time we long to move the stars to pity."—Gustave Flaubert, *Madame Bovary*

▶ Contents

▶ Foreword

When one speaks seriously and committedly of poetry—
when one truly *levels*—one speaks in the end of something
difficult to define, but which must in some way be acknowl-
edged: of the natural wildness from which poetry comes:
the unpredictable and untamable part of the human psyche:
pell-mell, throng-like and compulsive, an onrushing self-
proclaiming force, asserting its own order. Sometimes a pre-
carious balance is achieved: an equilibrium, even a serenity,
but if it is true poetry the wildness is there, underlying,
moiling and thrusting, never completely contained. In our
time an excessive concentration on analysis—linguistic, psy-
chological—and parallelism—sociological, historical—has,
as Conrad Aiken says, "silenced or enfeebled the more vital
and violent and generous element in poetry." That is the
general loss. I believe that in many if not all of us there is a
strong hunger for a return of this resource—or to it—and
that a veering toward the elemental, the unquestionable, is
having a result in the poetry, particularly the new poetry,
that we read.

Christiane Jacox Kyle moves hearteningly along this re-
turn; she is quiet and wild, neither a dry predictable wit nor
a professional maker of tiny surprises. She feels what she feels
and says so, drawing into her poems imaginative and strange
situations which, when lived-with, come to make a natural-
ness for themselves, and turn what we had thought of as the
ordinary world into another kind of strangeness that her in-
sight reorganizes and sets right. She begins with the circum-
stantial, a commitment to existence as it has been given to

her: to child-rearing, domestic labor, teaching, the natural landscape (including the firmament), and to a very clear kind of mysticism which is filled with awe and at the same time resigned, unquestioning:

> A seam of coal burns red within the sky.
> Hail spatters the ground. Far off, a coyote
> cries, the last voice from a mountainside.
> Two kestrels eye upwind. I take a cup
> from the wooden well. It's full of water
> where the sky blazes still. I lift the cup
> with both hands and drink as deeply as I can.

That is a true quenching; the poet drinks as though seized; drinks water, sky, and sun at the same time, there being no reason to hold back. The experience, the challenge, and the opportunity are *in* the writing: one says, I could do that, *like* that—no; I *will* do it.

It is the quiet, compulsive, private but not necessarily secret all-out, go-for-it, that is the distinguishing feature of Christiane Jacox Kyle's personality, and her poetry. Both are daring, honest, and above all believable. By means of her words, one is convinced beyond the words that these circumstances would call forth this reaction; the reader begins to take on the attitude the words make possible: he or she begins to learn, to live in a way not available before, to be taken up into the world in an enlargening and vital sweep.

There is more. Among the intenser experiences within

human possibility are those of dedicated and resourceful teachers; Jacox Kyle must surely be one of them. Her dramatic sense is strong, and is fully realized in her wonderful poem "The Second Language," as she moves through a forest-surrounded school in October, making essential connections between words and the world.

> "Tell me," one asks, "what is the word for the
> sound
> of quiet the forest will make?"
> "Quiet," I say.
> "But if the quiet is full of sound, birds, trees
> in the wind, water falling?"
> He is describing a man
> and a woman, how he imagines their life to be.

The poem then shifts, moving through the existences of human beings stultified by routine, by the absence of imagination, the lack of consequence in what they do. Some are the parents of children she teaches; from the child who has encountered the "second language" in the classroom and is now clothed in the light of new knowledge the parents will also take something hitherto unknown to them.

> The mother and father
> will gather the child clothed in light:
> the hush of wind, song, stars will take them,
> and their eyes will remember, their ears will tell
> the words of the forest breathing its dream . . .

That is not only true teaching—the truest, which is a radiance—but its statement, here, is also among the best new poetry to reach us, or so I am convinced.

I chose Christiane Jacox Kyle's book as the winner of the Yale Series of Younger Poets because of her clear, clean, and highly personal mysticism, the quiet and balance of her imagination, and her ability to articulate both sourced and sourceless joy. This latter may indeed have a source after all, come to think of it, as being something like—who can say it is not?—the moment when the Instigator of Genesis, coming from the ultimate Creation—the ultimate Wildness— looked and made out—beheld—what had been made, and saw that it was good. Good; all good.

JAMES DICKEY

▶ Acknowledgments

Acknowledgment is made to the following journals and anthologies for poems, or earlier versions of poems, which originally appeared in them:

Columbia Journal of Poetry and Fiction: "Dialogue in Jordan, Montana"

Deep Down Things: Poems of the Inland Pacific Northwest (Pullman: Washington State University Press, 1991): "Six Poetry Anthologies in the High School Library," "Sunday Afternoon," "The Second Language," "Oracle"

Jeopardy: "Stopping at a Roadside Rest in Beach, North Dakota," "His Wilderness"

The Malahat Review: "The Second Language"

Snapdragon: "Grandfather," "In a Dry Time"

Southern Poetry Review: "Creature of Dream," "Sunday Afternoon"

University of Portland Review: "To Copernicus," "In Good Time," "Letting Go"

Willow Springs: "Fire in Early Morning," "Oracle," "Six Poetry Anthologies in the High School Library," "The Green Place," "Paltiel Sings in the Field," "Night Walk at Thirty," "Walking a Father's Grave," "The Name of This Day," "Song for Crossing the Border"

Grateful acknowledgment is made to the University of Nebraska Press for permission to quote from John G. Neihardt, *Black Elk Speaks*.

Special thanks to James McAuley for his detailed criticism, to Françoise Kuester and Franz Schneider for their support, and to my parents and husband, Charles, for insisting that I keep on.

❱ The Second Language

For Mohammed Al-Abed

I walk through the classroom blazing with light.
In those hills beyond our one window the sun
burns the last of the morning fog. Already
it is October: Arabic, Japanese, Mexican, Yapi—
the students' eyes are careful as they write.

"Tell me," one asks, "what is the word for the sound
of quiet the forest will make?"
                              "Quiet," I say.
"But if the quiet is full of sound, birds, trees
in the wind, water falling?"
                              He is describing a man
and a woman, how he imagines their life to be.

There isn't a word for that silence, I answer,
and I think of the hundreds of words we have
no word for: *simpático, agape, ḥesed, nada,*
and the hundreds of homes where a man or a woman
returns each day, tired of work, tired
of the world, and has no word to come to
that means the quiet the forest makes saying
I am alive.
                So the child in the far room cries,
the wind cries, the pots rattle in the kitchen,
the wind rattles the bedroom where the man
and the woman lie locked in the anger of their lives.
And the silence between them is a thin scream

I

splitting open the round terrible silence
of the rising moon, and the light spills over the hills
where the fog lays down its head and sighs.

The man thinks of the absolute gray walls
where he works, and the woman thinks of the gray
faces of students who are American. What country
is this, the moon dragging the horizon, rumbling
its great and broken weight into the breast
of hills, hush of sky, hush of tender trees,
of stars brittle to the touch, the bears dancing
in the northern air? In the far room the child
cries, and they go to him.
                                   There moonlight
blankets his body, his arms flung over his head
in sleep the way a fisherman flings all
he is in a single cast into a pool where fish
bright as sudden stars lie dreaming
amid the rocks. The mother and father
will gather the child clothed in light:
the hush of wind, song, stars will take them,
and their eyes will remember, their ears will tell
the words of the forest breathing its dream:
it will be a language from before the moon
tore itself from the earth, the confusion of vapors,
the redolent splendor of dust in the spheres.

What is the word, what is the word? Hush. Hush. Hush.
We are learning a language that has no words,
of leaves, of laughter among leaves, an earth spinning
homeward through the broken heart of the spheres.

▶ Creature of Dream

June ascends like a specter: under
the swelling arch of the solstice,
our arms gripped round the great circle
of summer, we lift our heads and listen
for minnows canting their way downstream.
Between the walls of the Yellowstone
where Lewis and Clark journeyed, tracing
their names in shale, the crescent bodies
flicker and fail toward the Missouri
spilling across the wide Dakotas
through the heartland to where the waters
dissolve into the salt of a southern sea.

I watch you hoeing the earth,
your back alive with sweat, your arms
working the dry soil until it crumbles,
your lips rustling the air:
worm, spider, dragonfly, queen bee,
amid the lies we make to go on living.

Beneath this August sun that guides
a sliver of moon beneath its breast,
the land heaves back beyond itself,
the corn tasseled and still, the stalks
breathing that earth which once carried
delicate palm leaves, the first redwood,
a musty sea; the roots groan

toward bedrock, and cheat grass
ripples, knee deep and drying,
ready to churn into fire.

Today I stop thinking of names
for the child who surges within me,
its blind tongue curled back
to the waters of a warm and distant sea,
a pool without tides or moonlight:
its fingernails sure as a mollusk shell.

In March I dream I grow large
with child again: cornsilk hair,
eyeless and staring; my body aches
in the small places: hip-bone, groin,
the thin bones of a wren snapping.
Wanderer, Nomad, Voyager, be whole
under the spectral singing of the moon
though all our lies endure.

I drive all night; on my right the Great Bear
wheels and winds backwards like a restless eye.
Already old, the moon slides down the sky,
a late aurora sheathes the northern air.

I think of blind seals plummeting to where
blind waters sweep the lashes from their eyes.
Measure that distance. What can sanctify
the will to wander the moon's dark side? I swear

once there were those who knew how to live
in this world, drawing great shapes on bearskin,
cave walls: huge birds with hooked wings, a deft spear
lodged in a rib, each an amulet to give
a shape to fear. I explore the sky. I begin
with the first word. I name it Fear.

▶ Paltiel Sings in the Field

"Thereupon Ishobeth went and took
her away from her husband, Paltiel, son
of Laish."—2 Samuel 3:14

Her absence is December's sky
spread out in white grief
over every stalk and shriveled grape.

Bright were her beads on a rusting chain.
In this field, all light fails westward,
dragging her dark scent across the day.

And I lean at last with the oxen;
I would be the one before them;
Before their eyes the work is the way.

I hear the wind snap down the river.
My voice, this weathered splinter,
moors in the hollow of its song.
Can the wind bless a wound?

I know the wind that moves
is no wind at all,
but death's own bitter mouth.
What good is honey and wheat
against the gold of kings?

> I will go up to the city.
> I will make a new life.
> I will be smoke driven by wind.
> No god will enter here.

Tomorrow I will wake alone,
the wind's cold face on my far side,
and there will be no sound
of sweeping the hearth clean,
only my work in the dwindling days.

I will be worm,
I will be field mouse,
I will weep my sorrow,
and weeping, know the thin
cry of the sparrow
over these dark furrows.

▶ His Wilderness

For Solzhenitsyn

If you choose to walk in the glacial night
where tundra reaches beyond the steppe lands,
if you stand alone with your mouth numbed, feel it
      crack from inside you.

Keep your silence, waiting as ageless ice locks
all within, and even the wind's cry will be lost,
the hummocks gripped in the snow, their grasses
      stiffening slowly.

Search behind you. Watch for your footprints. Only
endless gray, that twilight, remains as stillness
piles in drifts around you. There none can follow.
      Snow will keep falling.

Go then, your tongue thick with the heat of fierce words.
Walk between those crevices choked with ice, and
singe the glacial heights with one thin and angry
      howl from the summit.

▶ Beasts

I should have been back
before nightfall. My headlights
are weak, angled too high
for the road. The way
was a slow way. I spoke
to the dark; I whispered
the small words. The answer
was crying. I breathed
a small song, and the wind
wound its long arms, calling
and calling, and the headlights
kept dimming, the road choking
with vines, and those beasts
I'd trusted to sleep in the shadows
crowd the road shuffling.
And I know you will worry
but they came when I called them,
they won't leave when I tell them.

▶ Anaconda Elementary: Mrs. Beechum's Fourth Grade

Lately I've begun to notice their hands
as they angle to their seats, just in time
to beat the daily bell. I watch them cramp
each finger around a pencil, the index
nudging a swollen steeple, their pale moons
rising up over the raw, ragged flesh.

In spite of my vigilance I never
catch their fingers seeking their mouths,
not even a nibble. They are busy
with crayons that spatter like rainbows,
they twirl wooden rulers like prayer beads,
pick apart the sniveling edge of a dress
for hours while their wooden eyes go on
watching mine for some glimmer of warning.

Oh I've taught them history: the brave dead
after bombings, never still, strewn in courtyards,
curled over the bare portals of churches
where one bell tolls the first hour. Here
the wind grows nervous, taps the sparse branches
and the trees are, sometimes, like lashes
slicing the wild white eye of the risen moon.

I tell no one, but there is evidence:
their lives gauged early in their little hands
they will not raise to answer for the midnight
rendezvous when they schemed—fists jammed
up into their mouths, eyes sealed shut—
the murders of brothers, or suicide,
some martyrdom reckoned to calm
for once the wild ringing of our hearts.

▶ Grandfather

First to go, he left on the sudden shift of dawn,
swung down the stairs and leapt the crest
of bursting hedges. His yawn

spit out the loss: at seventeen he believed
beyond the blur of Brooklyn's sun
that this day received

him and the sky was his. On bridges steeled against
the molten rising day, he learned the skill
of hard men, of birds, silence

hovering above the river. His blue eyes drilled
the sky, his fingers clenched the narrow air,
riveted by what he willed:

to see something come of hands, the scissor
of bone walking a lanky beam until the bird rose
from the man, and he was home.

Nerve slipped first: a hammer snapped and flung
across the dimming whine; then memory
left, a flapping wind that sprung

and shuffled him between years of tin lunch pails.
The union turkeys still would come Sundays
when he would begin his tales,

lose them, his hand drumming the couch, the meal done
his heart collapsing under the rising keel
of an admiring sun.

▶ Stopping at a Roadside Rest
in Beach, North Dakota

"Thunder and the West indicate a highly
sacred or powerful vision and signify
revelation, introspection, and deep
change."—Black Elk Speaks

This is no land I know from any map.
All day the air has bristled with thunder
and still there is no sign of oncoming
darkness in any quadrant of the sky.
Seven hundred miles ago, the gray cliffs
of St. Paul dropped down to a sheer prairie,
my car slipping through arroyos and grasses:
Blue Earth, Humboldt, Kadoka, Interior,
beads on a map I've devoted the day
to learning. At the Missouri, a wound
in the heaving hills, a nighthawk tumbled
out of the brimming blue of the noon sky.

Am I always at the edge of something
about to crumble? Once, two thousand miles
from here, I belonged to the sea, the incessant
curling of waves. I crouched in the high dunes,
gathering beach plums, the delicate shells
of animals I once could name. I leapt
the pure line where the wavering grasses
etched each day's wind in a new direction,
the wind tipping the dunes leeward each year.

A road sign points to a rest area:
I pull off and hear the trees beginning
to rustle, leaves in a light wind turning
toward the banks of the river. I get out

to read a sign nailed to a tree. It spells
this land's history: *first, over bedrock*
laid down six million years ago,
a broad swamp widened where the dawn
redwood flourished, the ginkgo, tall palm trees.
The water deepened to a sea. You still
may find, I read by the steady lash
of lightning now, *fossils of gastropods,*
the sturdy bivalve, squeezed between layers
of coal and shale. After the mountains rose,
the sea withdrew, leaving the rivers that etch
this land. I stumble down through wild plums
and reach the frothing river as thunder splits
the clouds. I shiver, slide out of my skin.

A seam of coal burns red within the sky.
Hail spatters the ground. Far off, a coyote
cries, the last voice from a mountainside.
Two kestrels eye upwind. I take a cup
from the wooden well. It's full of water
where the sky blazes still. I lift the cup
with both hands and drink as deeply as I can.

▶ Prayer for My Stepdaughter, Emily

We've come to swim the darkness, you and I.
The man who unites us, daughter, wife, tends
a small fire signaling the lake's edge,
knows enough of life and loss to let us be.
Alone, we enter a wall of cattails,
the water is cold, you are the one who beckons.
How we've both toiled toward this: fruit of love's
hard work without the buoyancy of flesh.

Night here as ever it was night, the moon
no graven image but hungry and bright
as a child endlessly rocking the sky. Was it
Diana who gave us the steady pulse of tides,
the water lapping this shore, the reliable
fires of your eyes? Men made those myths:
what can we count as ours? The night shepherds
us, the night abides, you at my side.

And the moon is a runaway child we meet
slipping down into water up to our waists.
We count, your ritual to make hard things
go easier, the muddy bottom sucking our feet,
old logs submerged, broken bottles, the refuse
from the street. We didn't choose our jealousies,
dealt us like a hand we'll never play exactly right.
We're past the reeds when you say ten.

The lake absolves us, swallows up our limbs,
except where the moon, steady in the west,
marks the wide, sure circles of your stroke
made out of muscle, longing, and of love.
I want you near as water slides and blesses thighs,
an old caress that names us both as female
not as myth: enduring arms, brave shoulders,
sweetness of waist and hip. Your face blooms,

a heron's slow ascending from the mist:
may this certain grace be yours to keep,
firm-hearted, strong against the tides shaping
the invisible shore. Count ten. Reshuffle the deck.
For here is a prayer you can hold if you want to,
since the moon is no goddess, but flesh and female,
and the water sweet, the darkness helpful,
salvation in the story you unmake, and make anew.

▶ Letting Go

The boy's drunk. Outside
they can hear his raw voice lift
and wail to the creosote sky.
His sobs shudder down tin walls
and anger splits his throat wide
as the gulch where his uncle,
close as a twin, lay for three
crumpled days. Tell him, they said,
Charlie's dead, *broken, silenced*
like a flapping jaw.

Scree down a cliff's sheer wall: he turns,
reeling against the bar, falls
against me, his tears stitched back
behind his eyes. Death was gravel
sliding from under me; I couldn't stay
the hawk's clear grasp of sky,
or hold the yellow blaze
of cottonwood that clutched
the river's desperate lie. I had
no words for him who stood there
losing his other lives, losing all
he owned, beating, beating
an old man's wrong against the wall.

▶ Night Walk at Thirty

In February when the land is still
half-locked in winter, the geese silent
and a few leaves hang like bats from the trees,
I walk down the old road to know
the night once more: wheel ruts choked with ice,
and a clear breeze light around me, my face a steady
mirror to the sky. Then I can find Orion,

the only one I could ever name, and I
curl in my father's arms, rocked on a ferry
crossing the Great South Bay, the wind
dancing spume in our faces while he nears
each star with a palm and names those
he knows well. Down the old road I slip

into farmlands where nothing is sure, not even
this grinning moon, nothing except the great
outlines of space and fields, bright rustle
of grass, the glint of mica. The road straightens

and I walk down an airstrip sliced out
of that luminous prairie, Otter Creek,
and dance through the blue and red lights
dazzling the runway. On nights like this

an old sorrow leaps to the bone,
sorrow for places lived in or loved well—

I can never leave that bowl of earth
near Flathead Lake, settled among the roaring trees
and all the universe at home. I lay on earth
I would never name, my eyes fixed on the long
approach of midnight, the immutable stars. And now

there is nothing to return to that hasn't been
made holy: this wind, these stars, this world
to the horizon, for all my ages.

▶ By What Remains

We stare down the canyon's open face.
What years blaze up in layered rock: sandstone,
shale, and silver beds of limestone trace
what once was living, held life, and now is known
only by what remains past life—all grace
of motion gone, the spiny creatures blown
across the continent, sand stiffened into stone.

Yet even now uneasy memories
unsettle us, thrust in a different view:
the rush of waters, warm and swollen seas,
and underneath, the river churning into
the rock bed, bearing small stones and huge trees,
carving the walls until the seas withdrew:
we reach toward where the river had driven through.

These are our bones, laid back to back. That image
stays; yet if we'd bend down, let our fingers play
along the rock, and scrape beneath its edge—
but we shift our feet, and turn, and look away
from what is rigid, fixed within its age,
and binds us to these bones which still betray
what once was flesh, but now is only clay.

The men keep searching the room
for the culprit. I tell them
electricity, those glowing coils
of wire, this ironing board
with the cedar frame, my coat
flung over the board. I don't say
I came home late, silly from a night
spent in song. They ask me how—

The dream told me: a scream
lunged from the cliff where I
slept in my skull, white winds
swept the ridge of my spine, shrieked
down the nerve ends. I remembered
my legs: the dream roared out a tunnel,
the smoke found the soft membranes,
sucking into those sockets
that glowed in the hallway.

I think it's morning but no light
shoulders its way here. The ironing board
staggers, its crippled legs bucking.
The coat is all gone, the green vine
blackened, limp arms dangle in the window,

and the dust keeps sifting through the tissues
of walls, the cells shriveling. My house,
my home, everything I touch turns away,
and a keening rises on a wind that keeps on
searching the bare coils of my brain.

November redeems itself not by what it
promises but by what it is. The chill grit
and grind of wind in shaky trees says night
shall sing no elegy for day. And the flight:
some slow-witted bird winces across the bitter blue.
The sky, so arrogant it would not stoop to
summer clouds, or patient spring rains, or even
lift one single autumn leaf in frozen
wonder, this sky electrified, shocked by desolate
etchings of trees along its face. The scarlet
sun stalks through the woods like a lonely
hunter, while November's blood runs only
to winter—sharp as spite, insatiable and deep
as those arctic winds that endlessly sweep
down through the canyons leading to sleep.

For Tucker

Look here: penciled between the thin
blue lines, his name, already smeared,
cancels the space in the margin

for *homeroom, date due,* the last year
he came to school. He'd stare at the ceiling,
his black eyes billowing with fear,

his hand tilted across a page, a wing
dragged down a steep alleyway
where I couldn't follow, or bring

my words to tame his fear. So I turned away
from his bent gait, the steady stink of beer,
and left him at the blackboard each day

while the factory hummed in his ears.
Gears he could understand, but the click
of words kept slipping from the wide sphere

of his mouth, and all he'd do was lick
the air, stare straight at me, and wheeze
like maimed birds might, seized in the flick

of wheels. But what was he doing with these
thick anthologies? What wings pitched
in the night, and with an eagle's ease,

moving in undulating arches, stitched
the widest sky? He's been dead two years;
they found him splayed in a roadside ditch—

Now the thin white lines of gravestones disappear
in winter. I curse the son of a bitch
who left him there. One by one, I burn each card, sear
his name, and keep the tongue of our secret fear.

▶ Walking a Father's Grave

For Tom

You bring daisies, still wet from the flower shop.
Your hands peel back the dead leaves, stems
without heads, dropping them onto the earth
near the edge of the grave.

All around in orchards, the men unfurl
the stiff canvas under the trees:
olives, black walnuts, the hidden seeds
clutter the white ground stretched
below the black branches.

You tell me a story of harvest:
the men in the families
beating the trees with great sticks
long into the early dusk.
We ate well, you tell me.

Yesterday, you held a photograph
of this man I'll never meet.
I noticed first how lean he was,
with your eyes, a dark bloom
curling across his face.
He was smiling, as if to say, *this
is enough,* a man
who didn't cry, spoke little,
knowing that words don't matter
when the grapes thicken the branches

and the slow September sun folds
over the hills and there's work
still to be done.

Tomorrow, we'll leave behind this week
of meals begun with wine, miles further
in memory than in fact: another of those
small separations in our lives that lead
to this place beyond the orchards
where grief tightens to the cold
slipknot of fear.

What can love affirm
that will not be altered here? I reach to touch your shoulder;
you hold out the daisies, now clean.
Without words, without tears, you smile.

▶ Calling

Notice how quickly the rain turns,
no longer exuberant, the closed cell
of warmth surrounding the planet
gone, gone the earth surrendering,
the steady effortless rhythm of days
and drops spattering the lilacs,
pure white, thick purple in furious bloom;
gone the rain right for whispers, faces flung open
under an artless sky, wet mouths, these wet hands;
and the grass widows bobbing beneath the rain:
oh love the one world, wet and warm,
made of a single sound.

How quietly the rain turns
to sullenness, a gray sky stooped
to a gray and reticent world;
now the predictable torrents where
the eaves have been left to rot,
the red wall of the barn stunned
into silence, rain robbing the hayloft of voices,
now the absent lowing of a cow, rain
breathing down insistent as asthma,
and somewhere, a lover calling,
father, mother, child, and the calling out:
oh let fall the impenetrable wall of clouds.

▶ DIALOGUE IN
JORDAN, MONTANA

Elva, I cradled that dying calf,
rocked it in my arms for an hour.
Our breath jerked in the air, both
of us lay wrapped in snow thick as flour.
Those cows had chewed the needles off

the trees again, their milk sour
in their bellies. God knows I tried
to keep them out of that pasture
all winter. That night I would've cried
out loud if I'd known how. You

would've cried, watching that white belly
heave against mine, the wind that scoured
his eyes. I wiped them and he
shuddered once. The wind climbed over
our bodies toward Miles City.

Oh John, your back curled against me, a curve
of moonlight from the window anchoring you:
what I see are thick shoulders, rib bones
rising on each breath, your sunken waist and hip
disappearing under the thick weight
of the blanket, your arm tucked and tight against
your chest, sleep and snow and winter winning again.

I hear the frost creep up the window pane.
Outside, a breeze stalks past the brittle rows
of last year's corn. I quiet the animal
roaming inside me, my arms twitching
before a sudden storm. When was it not
too late? When were you not tired and old
from keeping everything else alive?

The day we lost six calves, I came
home early, my fingers bitten
with blood, my voice locked up in shame
at the doorway. *"Don't let the cold in
John,"* your eyes bit off my name

before I reached you, your chin
dropped down, your small wrists
arched as you knit, I listened
as the fire trembled and hissed,
the click of the needles chilling

my skin. I looked out the window.
The calves were already hidden
from me and magpies and crows.
I brushed the snow from my mittens,
called the dogs, headed back into the snow.

I count what we have left, how many calves
what cows, which bull has shrunk to half
his weight. I subtract pounds of feed, the last
bales of hay, weigh loss against loss,
calculating between piles of laundry,
your shirts, your thin socks, the sheets
hanging in the stale heat of the fire.

What section are you in now? What fences
now need fixing? I watch your hands
gripping the rusting wire, your shadow
clinging, your eyes marking the last post
before you finish with the first.
You go back out there, quiet like a man.

▶ III. The Years

Look, my hands know what it is
to split frozen ground, to drive
those cedar posts, begging for calluses,
to winter deep in cold and survive
again and again, to burden my bones with this—

Elva, I raised this house for you
with my own hands. Land was cheap,
and cattle cheaper still. I knew
my weather, my fields, that crevice
past the pine trees where I drew

you down laughing into the drifts
we scattered, our bodies crystallized.
That night you taught me how to kiss
back the cold, remember? I
didn't know it would come to this.

You were the one I chose from all those other
silly boys. I knew what girls knew then:
forty moves will make you crazy, good fires
must be low, and kisses will not last
the winter long. What did we know of seasons then?
I watched the ice crawl up the cabin walls,

begin and end, begin again. I dreamed
six children while you stood and stared back out
the window at the calves huddled below
the restless pines. Has the wind entered there,
has the grass trembled in those blue shadows
where you took your tears year after year?

▶ IV. The Leaving

March slung down another foot of snow
before you left me. The blue rifts
deepened along the bitter row
of barbwire fence we strung in shifts
ten years ago. I don't know how

you made it through those drifts
that bucked and heaved their heavy backs
against your thighs. Wind clutched your fists
close to your chest, like the feed sacks
you carried, children to be kissed

before bedtime. I watched you go
from the window, shivered in the hiss
of half-light, my back to the stove,
my eyes aching through the mist
as you shriveled, a bird, a branch, a shadow.

They kept their silence, and with it mine,
those dumb beasts with their hot hearts,
mad-eyed and crazy with sorrow. Tell me,
if loss could speak, what words would lunge
thick-tongued across all kinds of weather?

Tell me: I've kept them crouched in the hollow
I carved in my heart, their soft bellies curled,
limp mouths turned against winter and wind—
I failed in that, and heard the wind sour
in scrub pine trees, drop snow like bullets
from a boy's quick gun. What was left outside
of Jordan howled. I closed my eyes and wept
under the scowling face of the wind.

▶ In a Dry Time

Those final days we lived inside the river:
dust gnawed the highest reach of wind.
We labored past the shrunken garden, a square
redeemed from a dying rancher's field where
July endured our presence. You grinned
as if to say, *I told you so, desire*

won't make a garden grow. You'd wait for me,
pity the exhausted lettuce gone to seed,
emaciated pods of beans the fat grubs
had seized. I'd kneel in dust, finger the nubs
of carrots shallowed between the indifferent weeds;
I knew last spring there was no certainty.

We scuffed along the path, drawing near, me
with my stubborn bare feet, you in sandals,
quiet in the chatter of cottonwood leaves,
invisible frogs that gulped the air like thieves.
We marked the ebb of April's flood, pale
stones nudging our feet. To be silent was easy

here, sunk knee-deep in water that flowed
like years between us. Words no longer mattered.
Minnows fled from our shadows. We clung
to ripples, the thin margin of comfort. Hunger
disappeared. Nearby, chokecherries stirred,
dropped down early, swollen in a hot wind's hold.

I loved you then the way a farmer heeds
a drought in April's breeze, and still works
the ground for seed; the way a women conceives
a child and begs that it will come to breathe;
the way a river winds between the rocks,
survives, turning the tender, silent weeds.

◗ We Two Who Are Sisters

It was death that drove me from you, not death
asleep on my lap, a wren bundled in kleenex,
the great oaks without requiem, only my wet
small hands lifting him up into the next
world, which didn't receive him—though I believed
in angels, heard their wings rustle, saw in the flash
of sun down the trees that God who breathed
the souls of creatures back from silence, from ash—

as it didn't receive you who didn't die,
but almost did, again and again.
Each time you go those times come back again:
my hands locked stiff between the earth and sky,
now, still, thirty years later, balancing as then,
love, death, faith, in the body of a brown, small wren.

▶ In Good Time

This time,
I'll take nothing with me.
Let the back seat be empty of voices,
the plates my grandmother gave to me,
their chatter bristling with peonies.
I won't listen to cookware,
the giggle of stainless steel.

I'll give away
the mossy green jars
I've saved for three summers.
Restless as children, they stray
from their boxes, dream of the wild plums
thickening on hot summer branches
before the winds come.

I'll abandon
this photo where I stand
dressed for a wedding, beside my young brother.
His voice skimming the silence
of midwestern prairies is always
faint on the wires.

This time
I'll leave everything
I thought I owned, in hope that
there will be reasons, in good time,
to return.

▶ The Green Place

I would conjure a chant tonight
to wrest tenderness from this dead
season, but what returns, insidious
as a late winter rain, is a boy
named Bobby who stood before me,
his right hand clenched to his hip.
He unfolded it like a rare gift
and turned his eyes down into silence.

That one claw cupped the air:
arcs of surgeon's black thread
held each finger fixed to the palm.
That hand had leapt into the air,
married a knife; the stiffening
flesh still throbbed and throbbed.

*"We were down at Jimtown, that honkey's bar,
last Saturday night, then Candy comes in."*
I remembered her, a small dark child
fixed like a wild animal to his heart.

"With another guy." He stared outside,
a branch bent to a starving sky. *"And then
this guy comes at me with a knife,
but first she runs at me and screams,
'Go to hell. No one would of married you.'"*

He wept, a small boy cradling his hand
on a winter day when no wind stirred,
and I spoke so that the words would light
on the last leaves burning on a branch
into the sun. I took up his hands, the healing
and the whole, small as my own: we held
the sky between us while the drenched
clear light moved on a winter field.

▶ The Name of This Day

For Sarah Youngblood (1929–1980)

In another age no neighbor would have lost
a moment to carry the news that death
had devoured you. In my garden, there'd be time
to lift my hands full of burst Shooting Stars,
and mark how those crimson petals travel
nowhere, then drop to earth in one brief day.

But news circuits the wrong roads today.
Idling at the checkout stand, I read we've lost
miners in Appalachia, I skim the deaths
of Atlanta's children, passing the time
with their faces, their lives. One by one, stars
go blind:
                 for years whenever I traveled

I recalled your name, how you told us *travel*
wide continents, your white hair a lamp each day
navigating the room, coaxing us to loose
"Heaven blazing into the head." Even dying
you quickened your course, but found time
to call each small flame to explode like stars.

Now this newspaper clipping with a red star
beside your name. How I should have traveled
to beat that month-old news, to meet that day
that dropped like a broken weight. What hope is loss
that grieves alone and late?

                    Your people knew death,
    how it changed as soldiers hounded them in winter time,

    without land to consecrate the dead or time
    to lift the children up to see red stars
    marking the Oklahoma snow. Sorrow traverses
    the hills you climbed: you remembered yesterday,
    that young tribe hiding out in shame, lost
    Pleiades, so learned another face of death

    but with the same name.
                            What route does death
    like best? This broad leap across time
    cancels all we know of motion, for stars
    burn out a billion years too late, travel
    the path of Heisenberg's Law: running by day
    we reckon our course, but can't reckon with loss.

    The fires of stars and words are never lost.
    Blood grows strong as it flowers toward death.
    Matter's neither gained nor lost in time:
    You knew all this and more: become a star
    blazing at noon from my garden; travel
    your galaxy knowing the name of this day.

Now it begins. The sun plunges down
in circles through the trees. It spills
over stiff limbs, the fire crown
rising: a burning of the hills.

Now out of the heart something thrusts
deep into the brain, jamming up
against the skull, driving black gusts
of wind until the thin walls drop

wide open, and the winds rush
out over the hills in spasms.
Listen:
        Beyond the charred stumps the hush,
the fog, are crawling toward the chasm.

Because I am neither wife
nor lover, I contain my hands,
let one cradle my forehead
as I would cradle yours;
the other drops to my knee,
kneading the round bone, stiff
from sitting at this odd angle.
You don't have to say
this talk makes you tired,
or that the woman you should love
and the woman you do
are not the same. Yawning,
you blame a cold drizzle
in the middle of May. Outside
the window, forsythia bloom
like impetuous girls
and I contain my thoughts
as I would fold your thin arms
into mine. Because I am neither
brave nor foolish, I don't say
what I want. You are gruff
with your son, and the rain
is like a mute hand at the window.

▶ Street Psalm

It's Elva I think of tonight,
God of the maimed, the hump-backed, sway-backed, that woman
whose blood followed her everywhere, the blind
man's white planets where there might have been eyes,
all that twisted flesh, miracle of metamorphosis,
binding and unbinding its sheets at the public bath,
left to tell and not tell of the heart:

Oh knot of heart that will not be untied

And not speaking, speaking, the stump a mouth,
the mouth convulsing the air along a dusty road,
a crying out unto the rooftops at sunset,
the swallows faltering, wing and heartbeat pinning the sky,
without need, without fault, without guilt or guile.

God by whom this woman dwelt all her days
in two rooms with a man dying inward
slowly of the booze and a busted gut,
and when he died without a wallet in the VA,
she called him by name, cried out if he knew
the hurled half-empty glass, the steady downpour
of wrath, was something other than this:
love twisted into the flesh of rage.

And who herself not six months later,
lay down in a warm bath and read
a borrowed romance that wouldn't tell
of wristbone, backbone buckled with age,
lay down and heard her own heart rend in half
and wasn't found until the next day
while the waters rose and spilled from a private grave:

Oh knot of heart that cannot be untied

So her one remaining relative told me
on an afternoon in December
when the swallow nests were covered with snow,
and the wind howled the temple down,
my body rocking itself into the night.

And now it is you God of the broken-backed,
the white-eyed bleeders and screamers,
those multiple shapes which the body breathes,
whose hand holds the sparrow's thin throat,
which shape do you take? From out of what mouth
making its slow way down Jerusalem's streets
have we heard your cry?

▶ The Argument

So many days spent tracking the desert,
the white cliffs, so many checking the map,
reading the wind, birds scratching the dirt,
the slow shiver of light fingering the back
of the neck; so much blood and sinew and heart
spent in wild hope, stunned in the black
cavern air, dripping with sweat, under each heel
old bones: the promise, but never the fact

of gems. To come only to this, to come
to nothing. To kneel down in mud and cry
empty, empty, empty, and hear the stunned
shrieks of bats ring out in wild delirium,
the heart roaring outloud, the cold breath of sapphire
invisible, flowering underground.

I have come home,
the black asphalt spilling
over the sinuous hills,
my throat leaning, embracing
the slow curve of buttes, the steady
wire-worn fences, sage
a tenuous green. Houses
shrink back, the tin blackening.

Burnt scoria dust
between my lips, my teeth
gone rusty, my words
clumsy: this spirit curls
back into silence, gathers
a few stones from a ravine,
those small fingers rubbing
each into dust songs,
spelling their secrets.

It is the space of hawks
that frightens me, spitting
flecks of some ancient flood,
stones a thousand years wiser
than I. The wind breaks
into faces; a single car
slips between the hills.

❯ The Music Box

I studied it closely, guessing at oak
or birch, although a more accomplished eye
than mine had said the only certainty
was time had been lenient. One hurried stroke
had cracked the box. It held, though forests grew
wildly along the crest of broken vines.
Patterns sketched in troubled lines
were left to fade, like something never new.

The song that rose in pieces from that wood,
did it hesitate, as if it could call
back the artist's curse, the stubborn awl
he hurled away; or had it understood
always, only the unsuspicious ear
would know the song, simple, whole, and clear?

❯ Fire Stolen from Heaven

Beethoven conducts his Ninth
Symphony in Vienna

Fussing with chairs, the orchestra assembles
in dim, amber light. Then their Beethoven,
their angel of madness, orbits the small stage,
hovering near the podium. Applause trembles
polite, aristocratic, rippling the man
who, though approaching middle age,
sulks through Vienna's streets without a coat,
hungry, drenched in rain, blessed and remote.

Casting his arms to the gilded eaves,
his hair already blown back into waves,
he calls his violins, his cellos, out
from dusk, a rustling in the summer leaves.
The earth answers with trumpets, solid, grave
in counterpoint, weaving sweetness without
light; ascending and falling, they soar
in his bold weather as he grows more

and more relentless, breaching obsidian
clouds, rifting through thunder, the golden air—
his bones break into wings, and, as the musicians
lift their bows, prepare to end, the women
turn to the men, grow pale, and all stare
in horror as the deaf man, the magician
keeps on lashing the air, his eyes
fixed on a measure all light denies.

The blazing arcs of burly arms call back
the flutes, the violins, the voice of horns
back from air, back from silence where all song
has disappeared to rage against the black
and savage sun. The concert master warns
them all with a whisper, *this is all wrong,*
and grasping the wings that slowly fall, now
turns him to face the audience, and bow.

▶ Parting

For Lesa

I could tell you the names for other countries,
their mountain ranges, their secret seas,
or the name of a home you once lived in,
Four Lakes, where the fog set in each spring.
There the landlord brought you steaks, solicitations,
drunk ramblings, though he meant no harm by these.
Neighbor, friend, stranger, we took our bread
together and separately, and you left, the white
picket fence graying through the slow wash of seasons:
red apple, green asparagus, gray willow trees.
I hold to the bittersweet breath of memory,

but cannot give you a name for this:
the young pup you took in, black and quivering,
part Saint Bernard, part of some wild breed,
and kept awhile, then sent away to another home
so you could leave. Forgive this brooding, when young
like you I didn't know the ache of motion,
the desire for one blessed fixity,
familiar and certain as the return each year
of the soft, gray blossoms on the willow tree.

The whole town is silver cast in ice,
winds tipping the black roots skyward,
brittle buds clattering on sidewalks
and bursting in a sudden change of weather.

Yesterday's sleet is water down the wells;
the slush heaps up in mountains on the street.
Outside the town, the hills are white and clean.
The season doesn't matter; they still could be

amber or brown or green. They ride the crest
of a single wave, and roll their shoulders
side by side; each year stands of new trees
shoot up from where the wet ground cleaves.

Inside the clock ticks forward on the wall.
The lone cat moves from where the fire's spent.
We cannot hear the steady rush of rain.
We roll the flowered sheets back from the bed,

and rock these hills, anchored by what we know,
crouched in the little valleys as each knee
gains a hold on earth where it's easy
to forget if anything was wholly ours.

Dear Carrie Lou,
        We've turned emigrant now,
shackled ourselves to wetlands. Mist riddles my eyes;
it seeps down through the grottoes beneath a soft earth.
The glaciers are dying here. We're as distant from sage
and sorrow as those antique dreams of Black Elk,
learning new words to steal what our memories have kept
from us.
        I keep thumbing your letter like sweet pieces
of cedar. I search for a prayer. I wish I could tell you
it's better not to be hard. Lord knows
we've both spent years fighting that river,
you for better reasons, watching your friends
drown on their barstools, crack open their heads
on windshields, gravity.
        I wish I could say, *be hard,*
don't think, the way you taught me to shoot pool;
consecrate your life to something as simple
as six Olys, a clean cue stick, and the eight ball
pocketed into the river under the table waiting
for us in every bar.
        When we go home, we'll carry the rain,
the river, these words, and our eyes at flood tide, those
we have ransomed for learning.
              Yours,   Chris

▶ To Copernicus

And you, Copernicus, do you still search
the howling tunnels of the spheres for bearings
we might yet command when time's unreasoned lurch

astounds us? There nothing has been known to sing
unless within the heart the voice were wholly blind:
The sudden arching of a nighthawk's wing

negates the moon, and those stars that lurk behind
the darkest reaches of each spinning head
move in solitude on journeys that wind

the wild, white heavens no charts designed. Naked
eyes can burn through scores of suns, cause
day to fly, and night to be one-sided,

while within the thinnest breath of time, the pause
between daylight and dusk, a galaxy
is lost—that's all there is, or ever was—

no screaming equations, no cold decree,
only the buzzing void, the longest cave: there
the bat beats its paper wings, knows only
the walls that close in by pulsing in mid-air.

So sleep now weary poet, but look, if only
one more time, outside, and find the familiar
star that follows you in harmony,
wherever you go, wherever you are.